My name is ______________________

I am ________ years old.

My favourite number is ______.

Draw some things you know about your favourite number.

Numbers 0 to 20

0 zero 0 zero

1 one 1 one

2 two 2 two

3 three 3 three

4 four 4 four

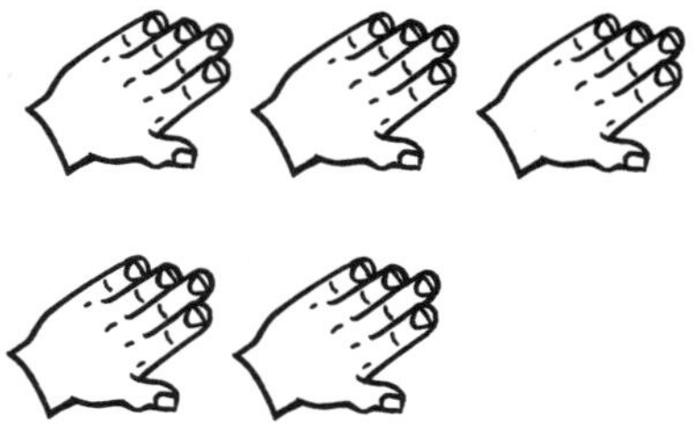

5 five 5 five

6 six 6 six

7 seven 7 seven

8 eight 8 eight

9 nine 9 nine

10 ten 10 ten

11 eleven 11 eleven

12 twelve 12 twelve

13 thirteen 13 thirteen

14 fourteen 14 fourteen

15 fifteen 15 fifteen

16 sixteen 16 sixteen

17 seventeen 17 seventeen

18 eighteen 18 eighteen

19 nineteen 19 nineteen

20 twenty 20 twenty

Channel.

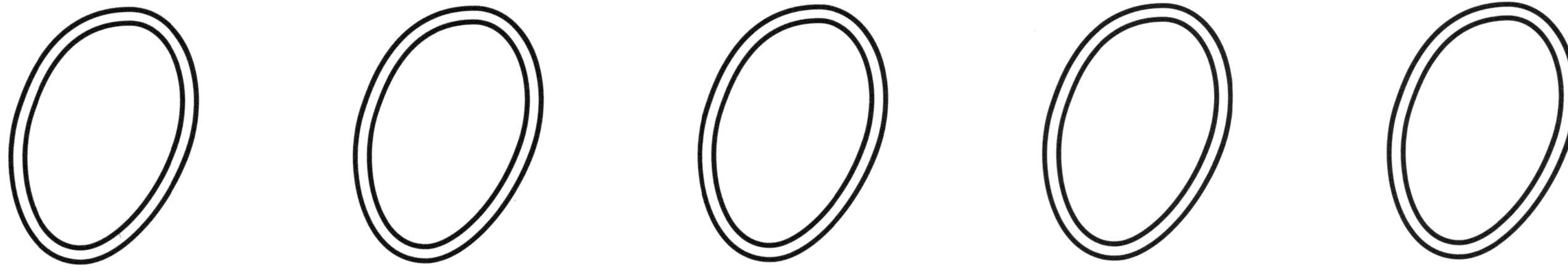

Trace over.

Trace over.

zero zero zero

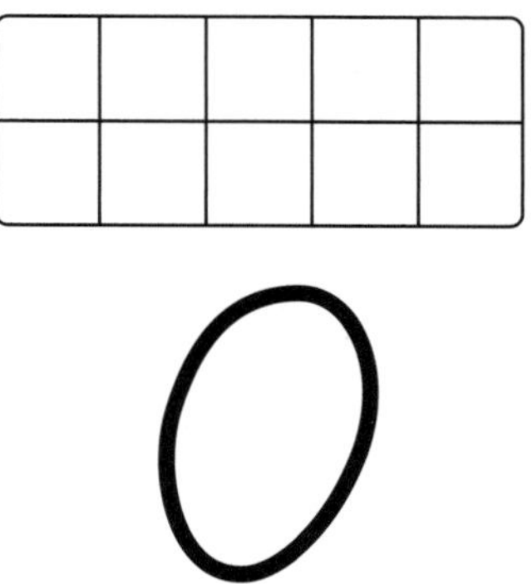

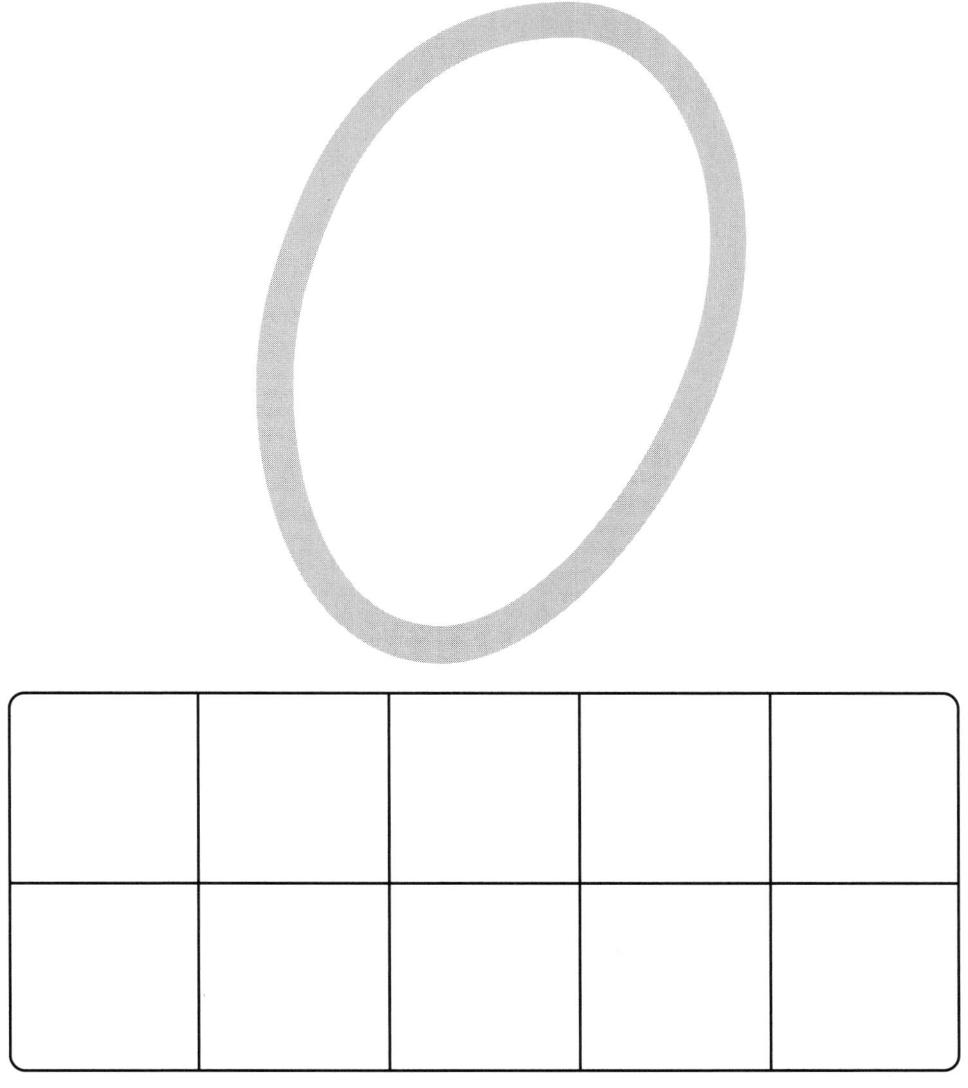

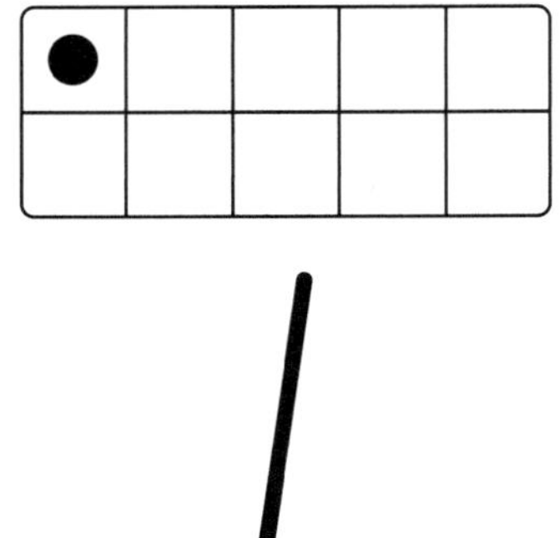

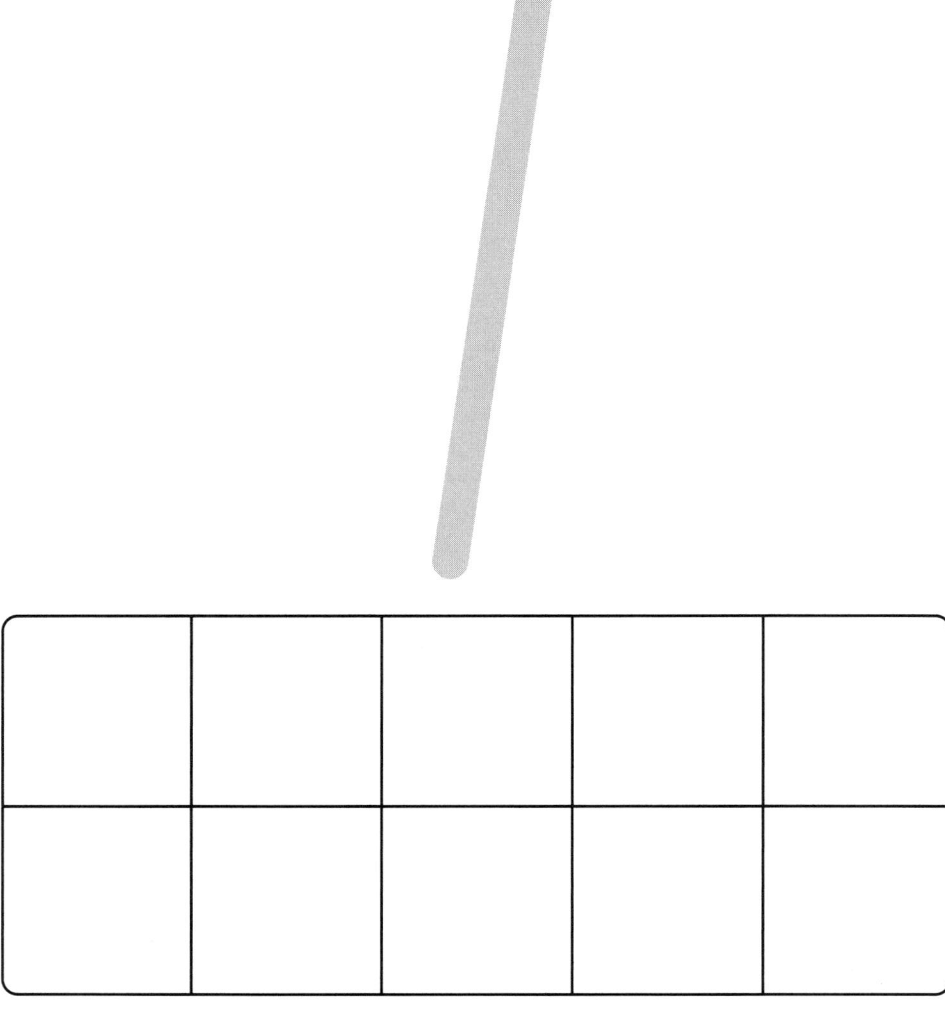

Channel.

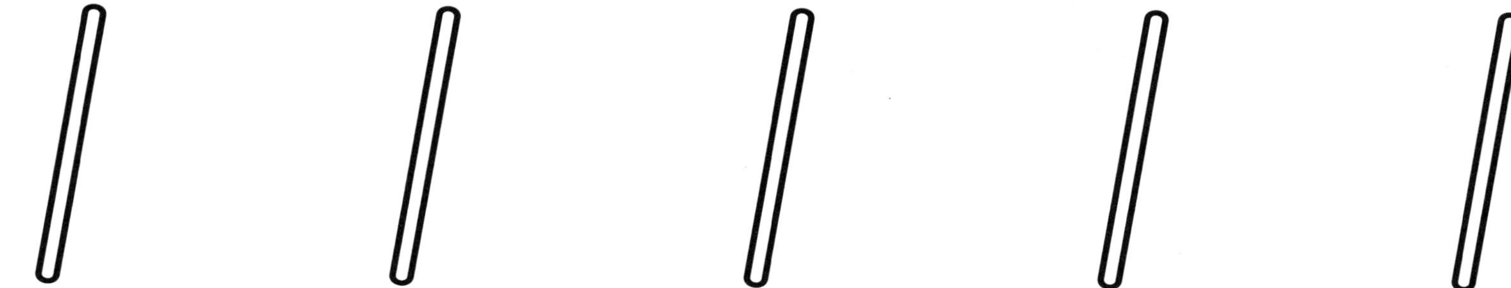

Trace over.

Trace over.

Colour 1 apple.

Colour the 1st pear green.

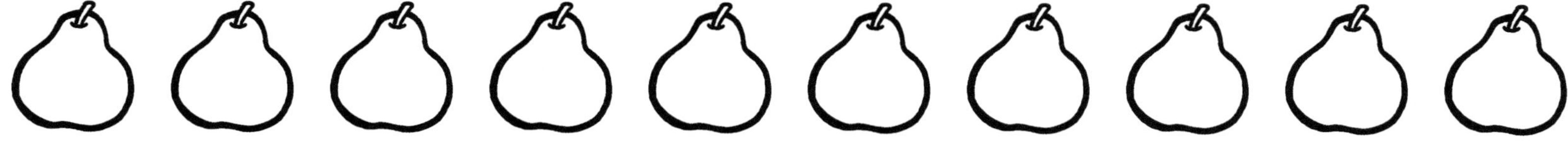

Channel.

Trace over.

Trace over.

Colour 2 bikes.

Colour the 2nd scooter red.

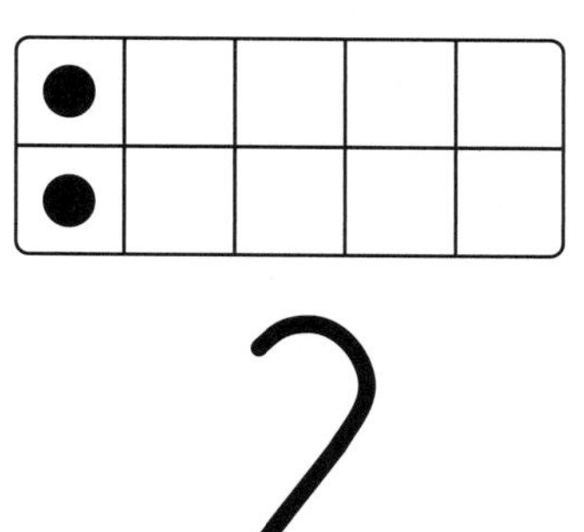

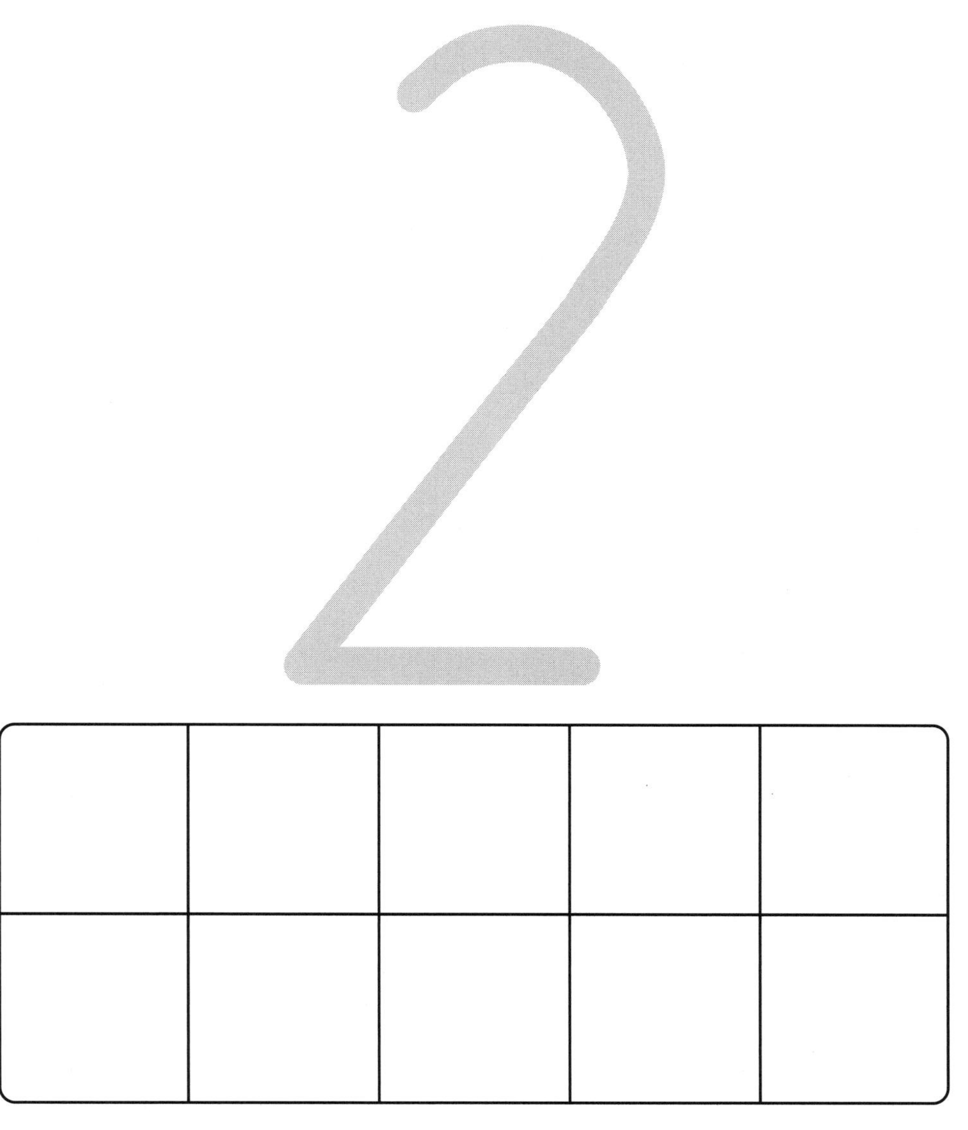

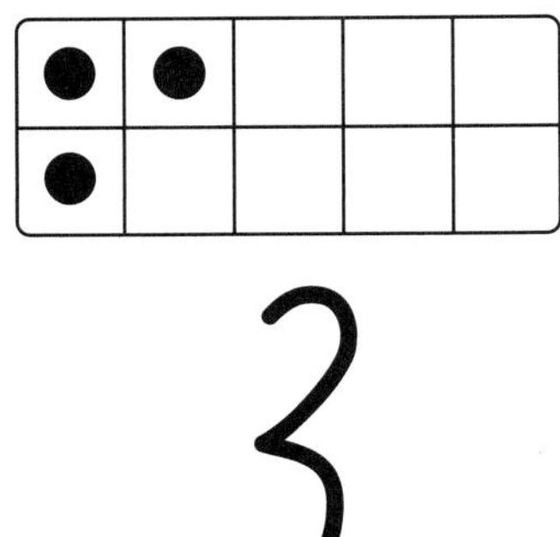

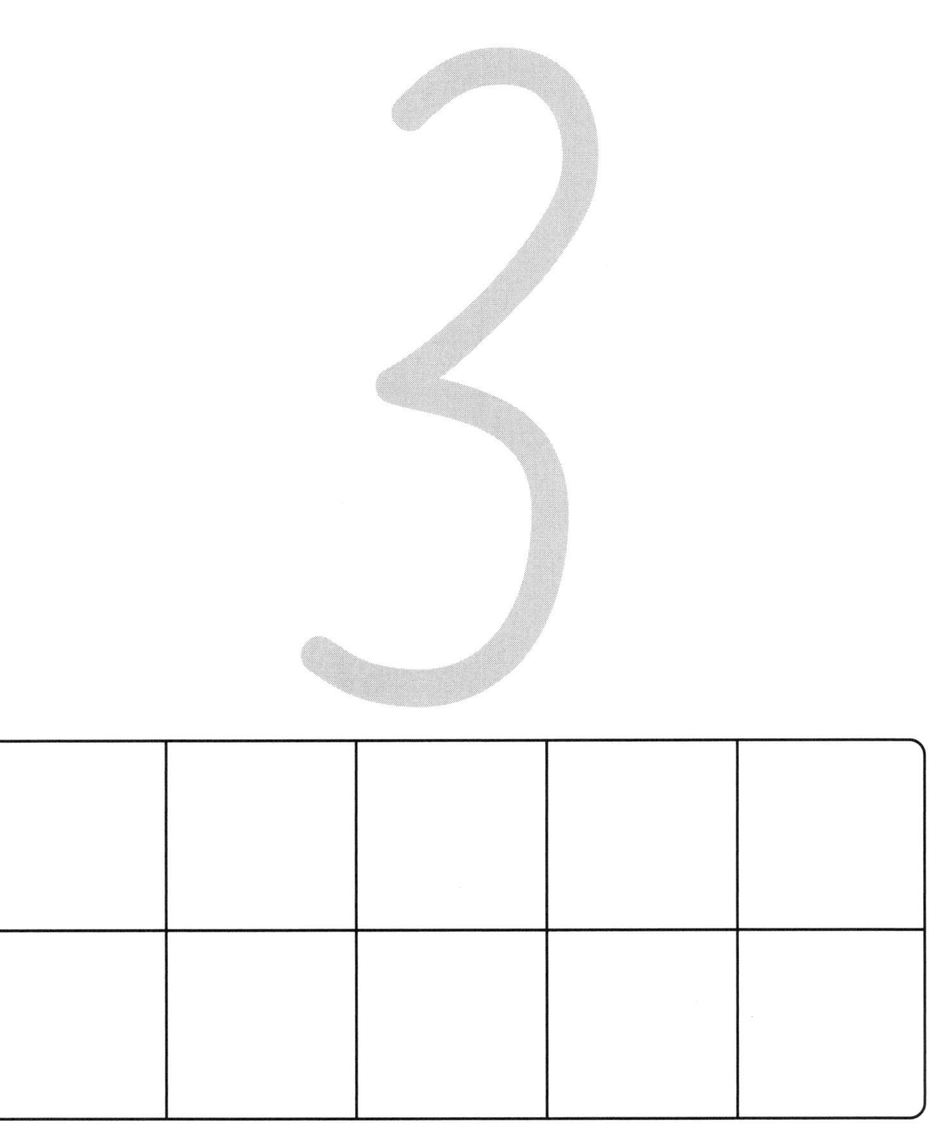

Channel.

Trace over.

3 3 3 3 3

Trace over.

three three three

Colour 3 clovers.

Colour the 3rd leaf orange.

Channel.

Trace over.

4 4 4 4 4

Trace over.

four four four

Colour 4 cats.

Colour the 4th dog brown.

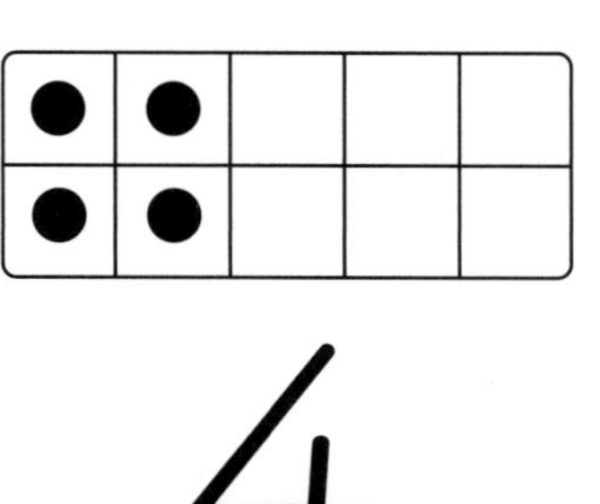

4

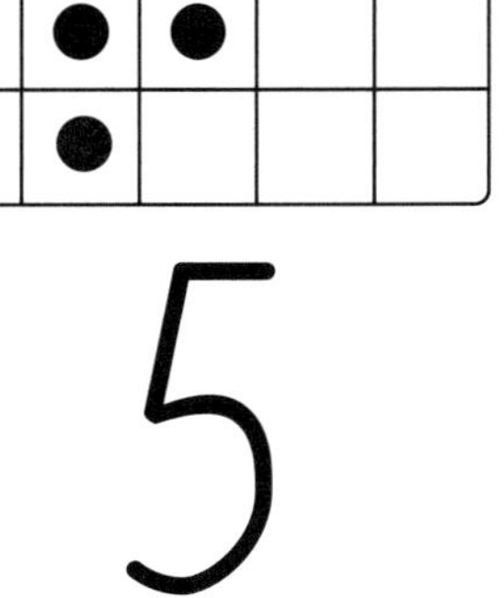

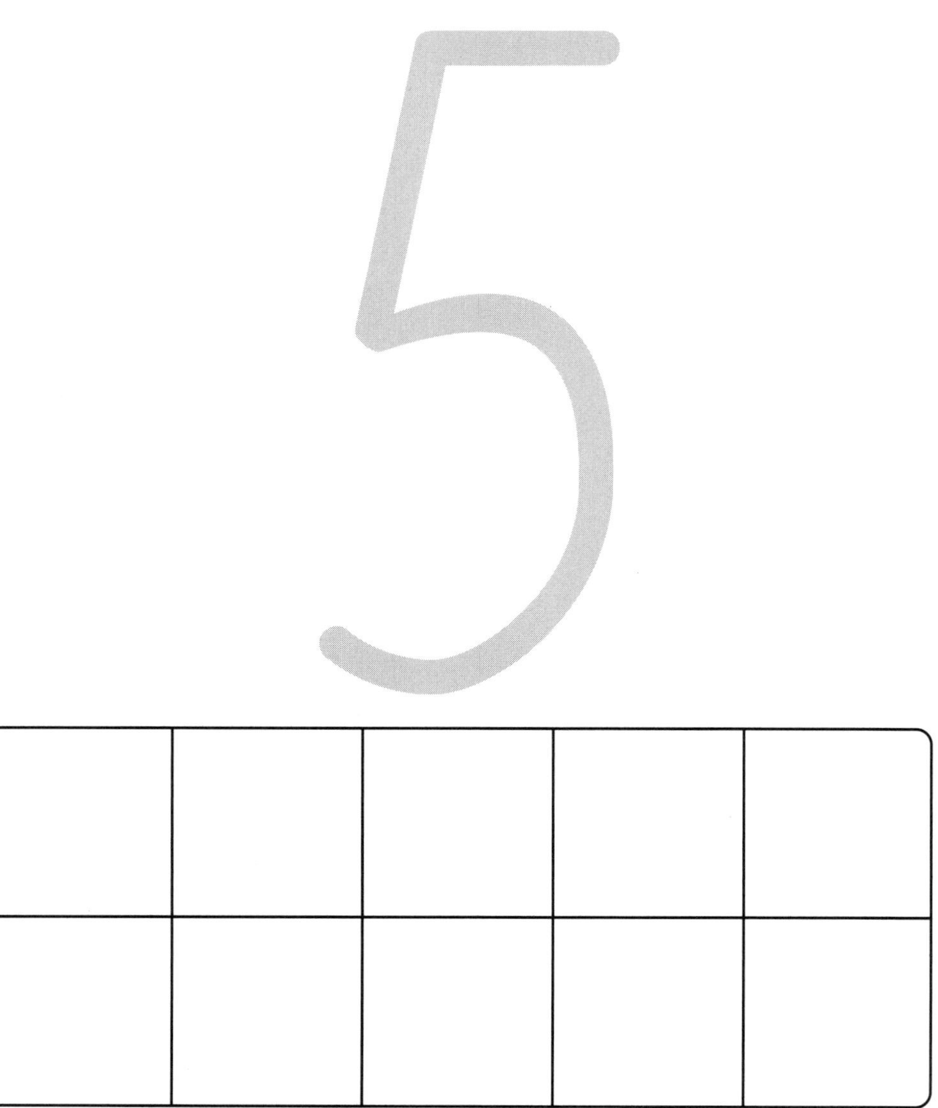

Channel.

5 5 5 5 5

Trace over.

5 5 5 5 5

Trace over.

five five five

Colour 5 hands.

Colour the 5th starfish blue.

Channel.

Trace over.

Trace over.

six six six

Colour 6 ants.

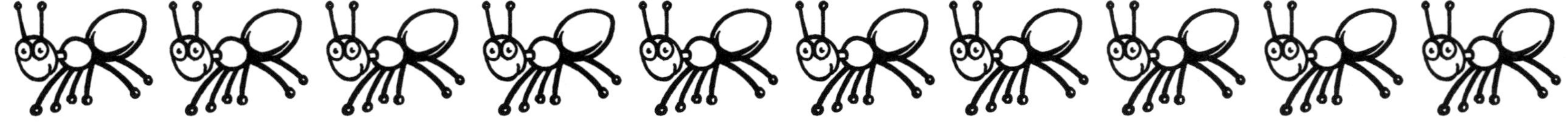

Colour the 6th bee yellow.

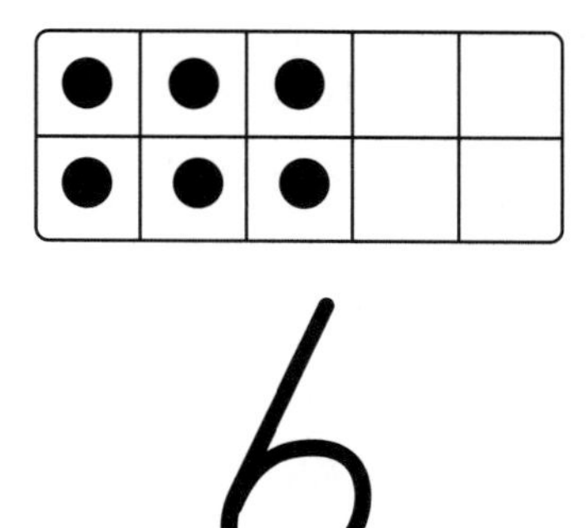

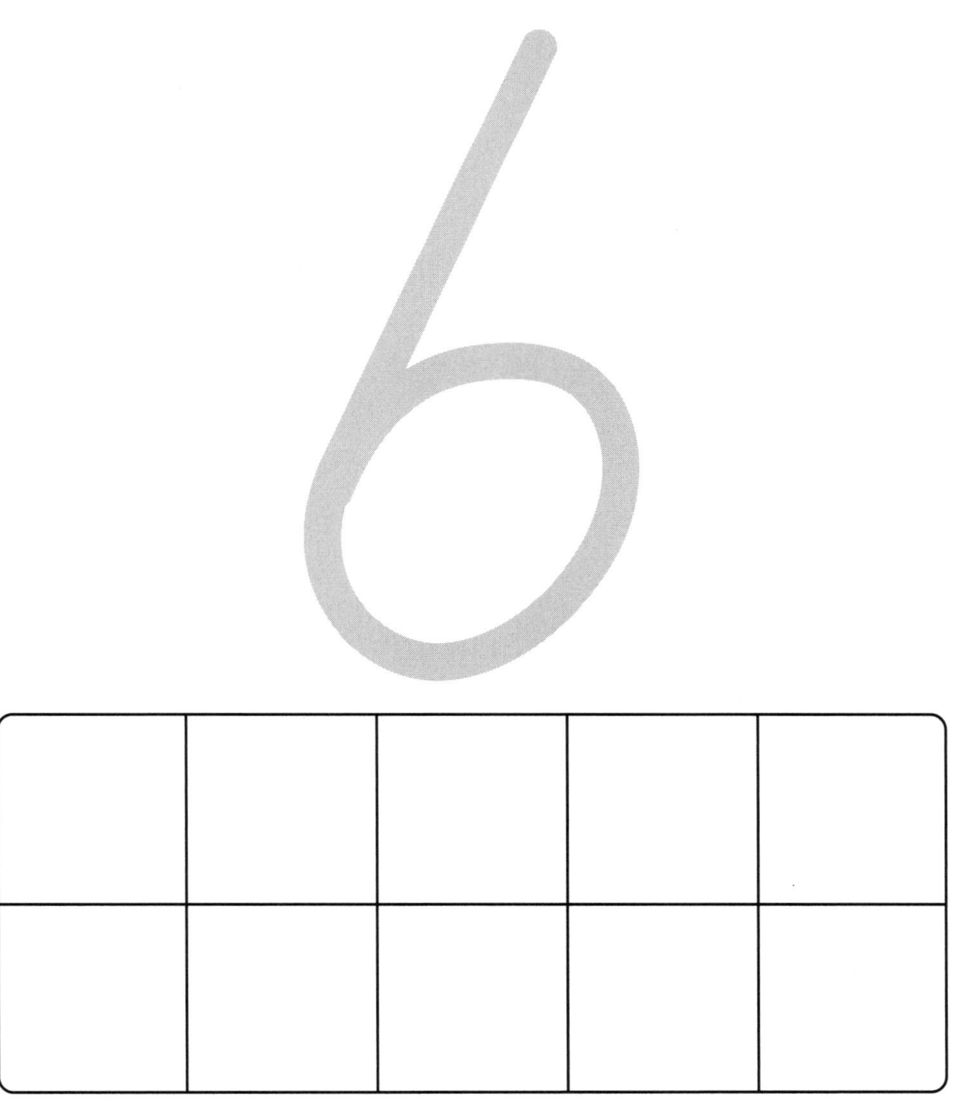

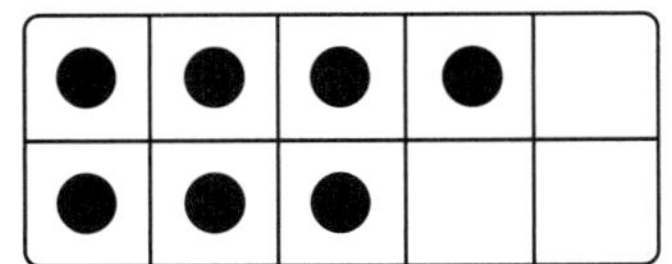

7

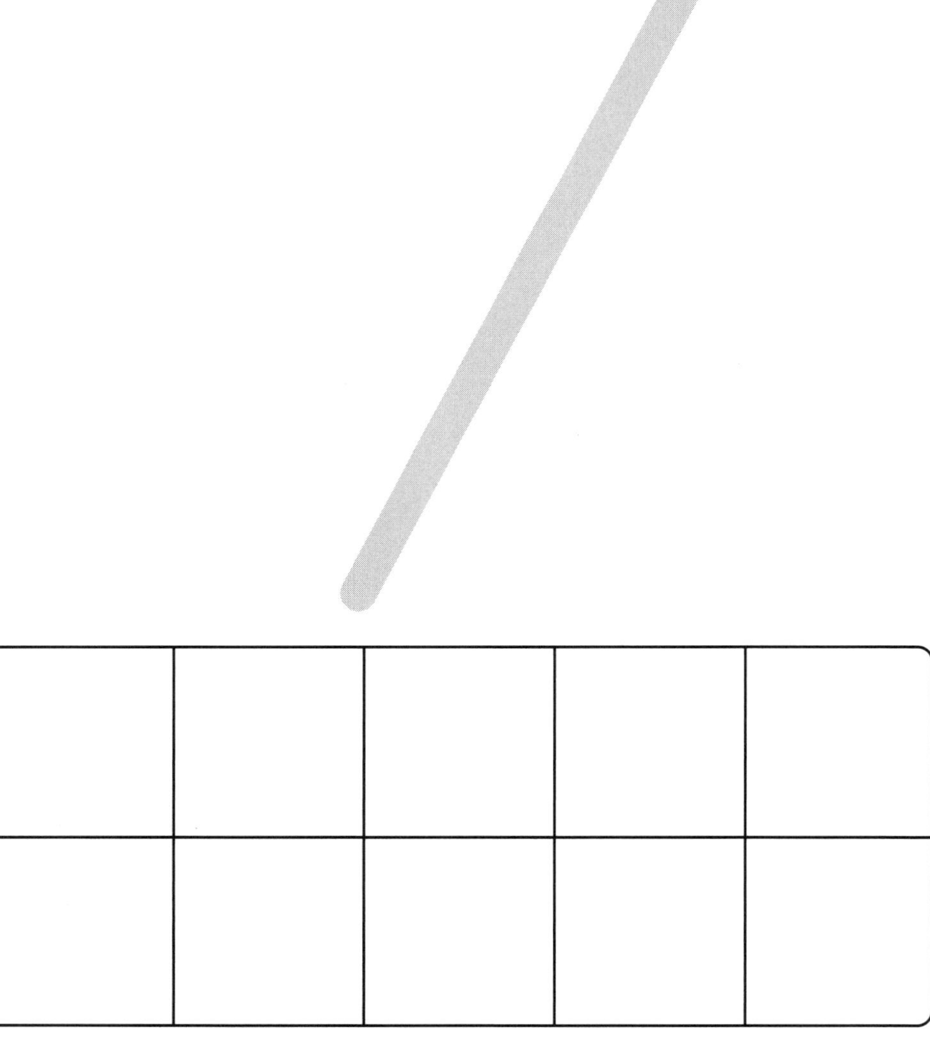

Channel.

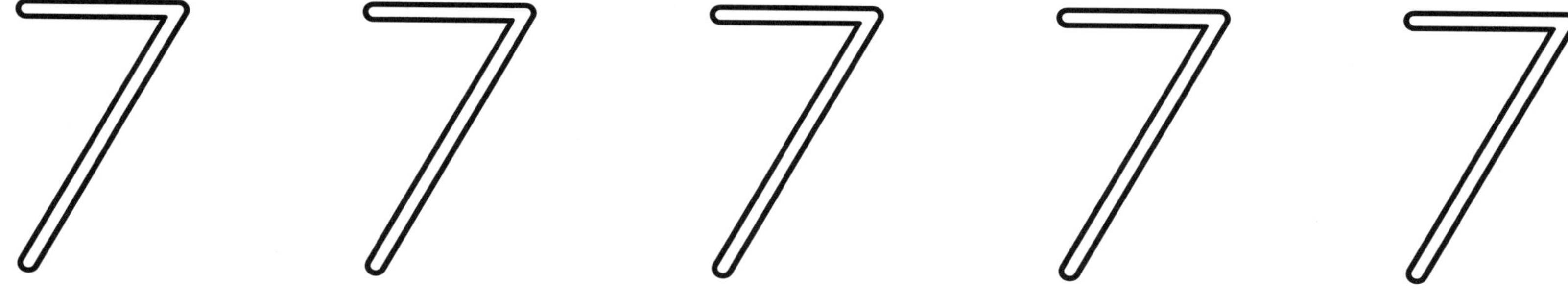

Trace over.

7 7 7 7 7

Trace over.

seven seven seven

Colour 7 cakes.

Colour the 7th cookie pink.

Channel.

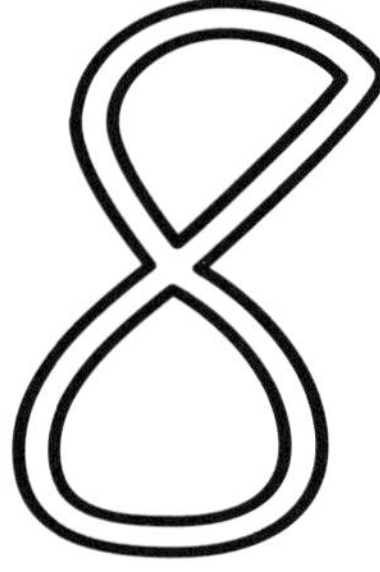    

Trace over.

8 8 8 8 8

Trace over.

eight eight eight

Colour 8 spiders.

Colour the 8th octopus black.

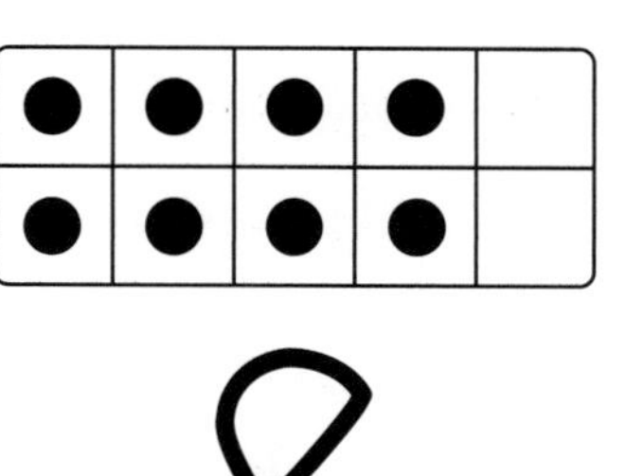

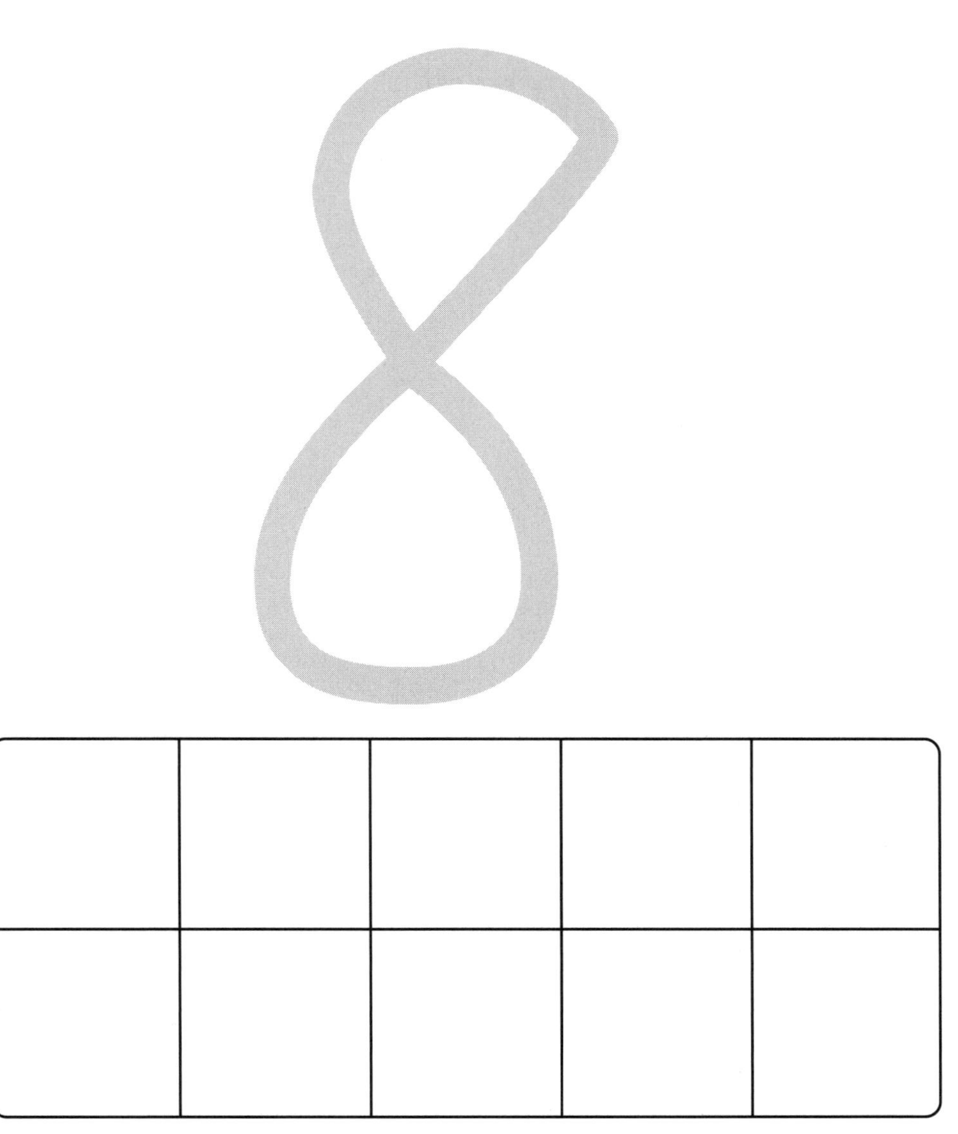

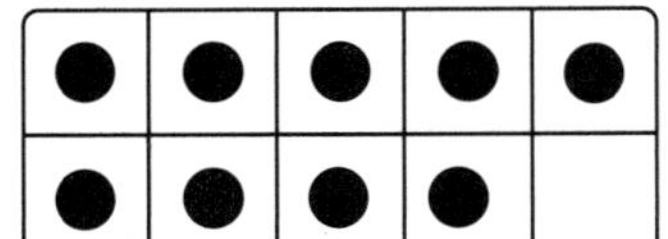

9

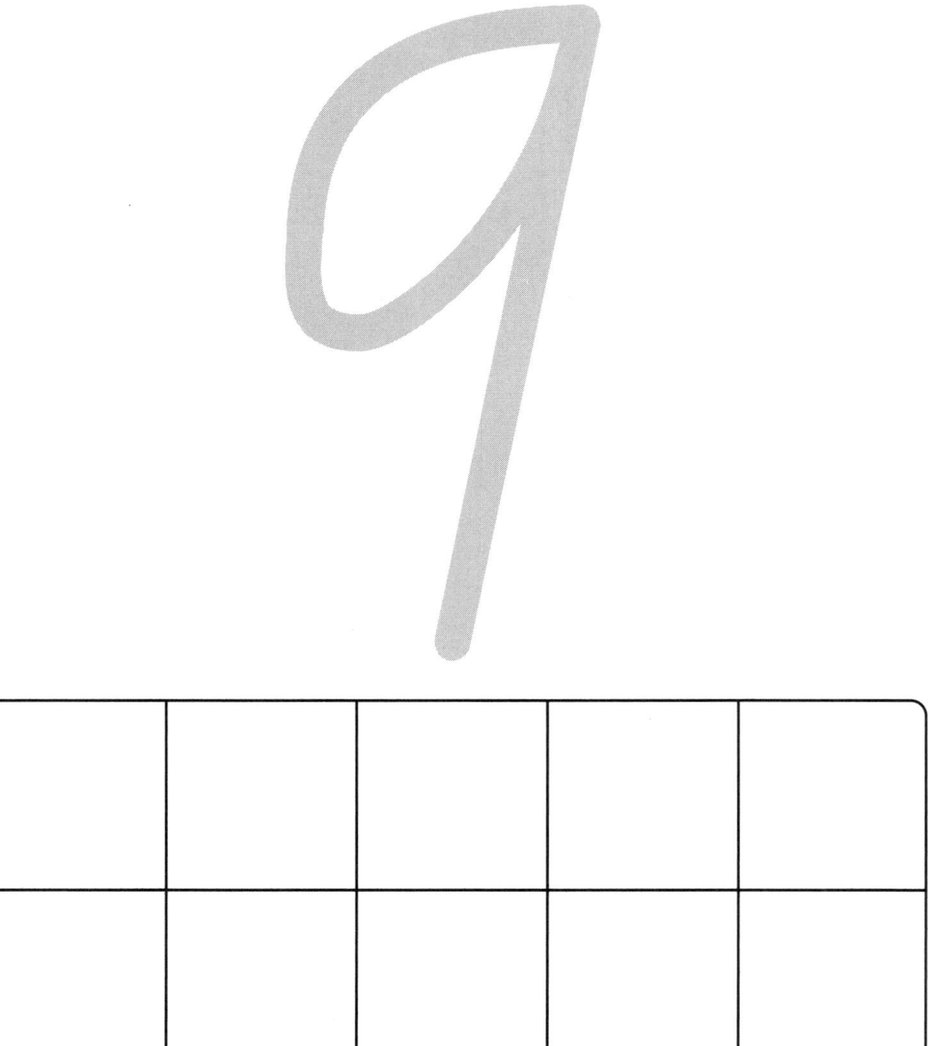

Channel.

  9 9 9

Trace over.

9 9 9 9 9

Trace over.

nine nine nine

Colour 9 flowers.

Colour the 9th flower red.

Channel.

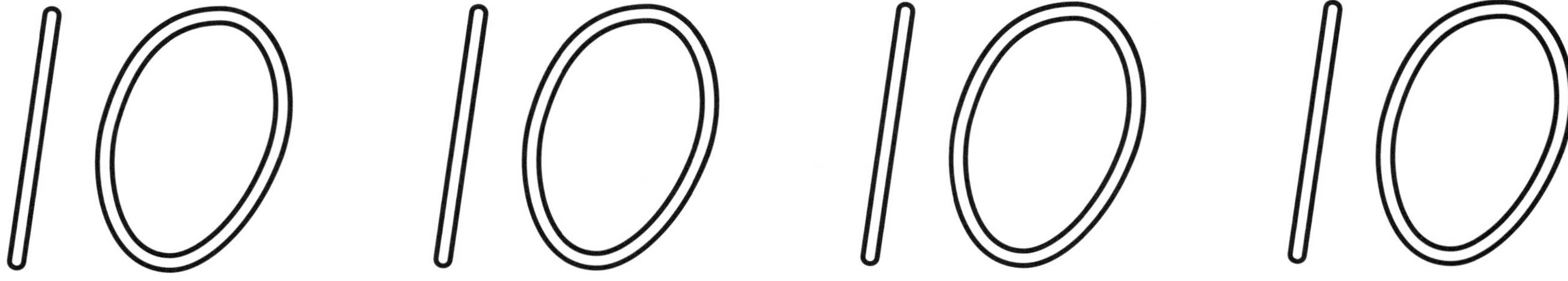

Trace over.

10 10 10 10

Trace over.

ten ten ten

Colour 10 jellyfish.

Colour the 10th seahorse blue.

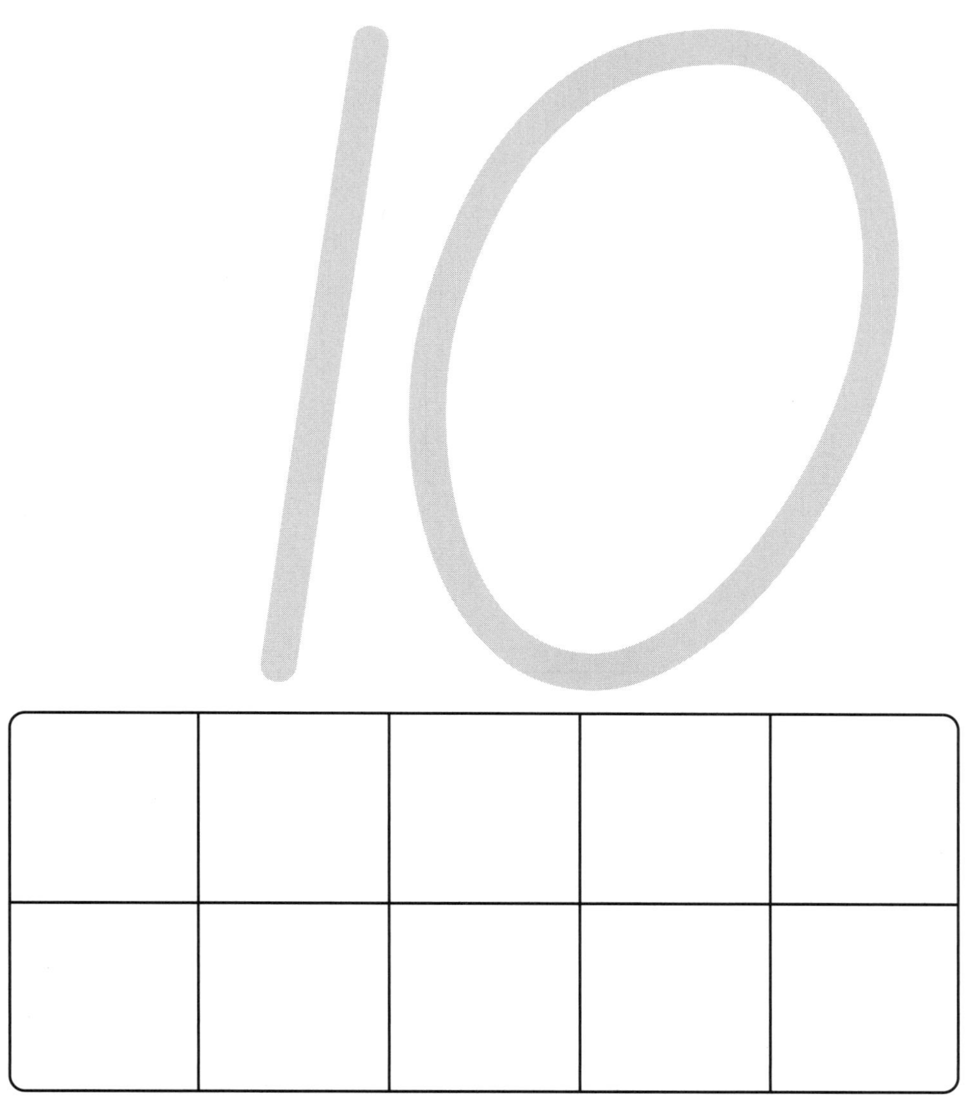

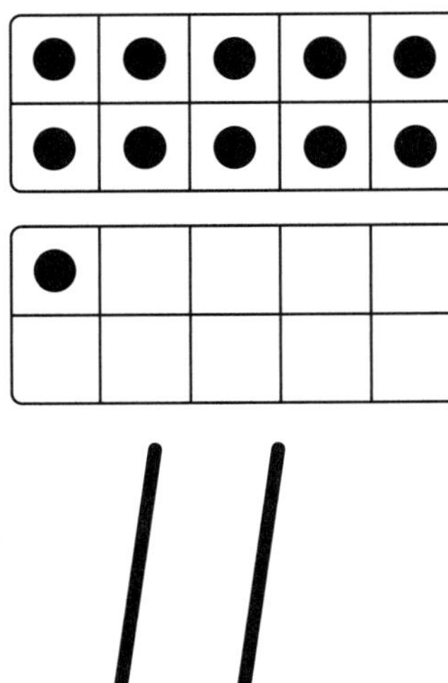

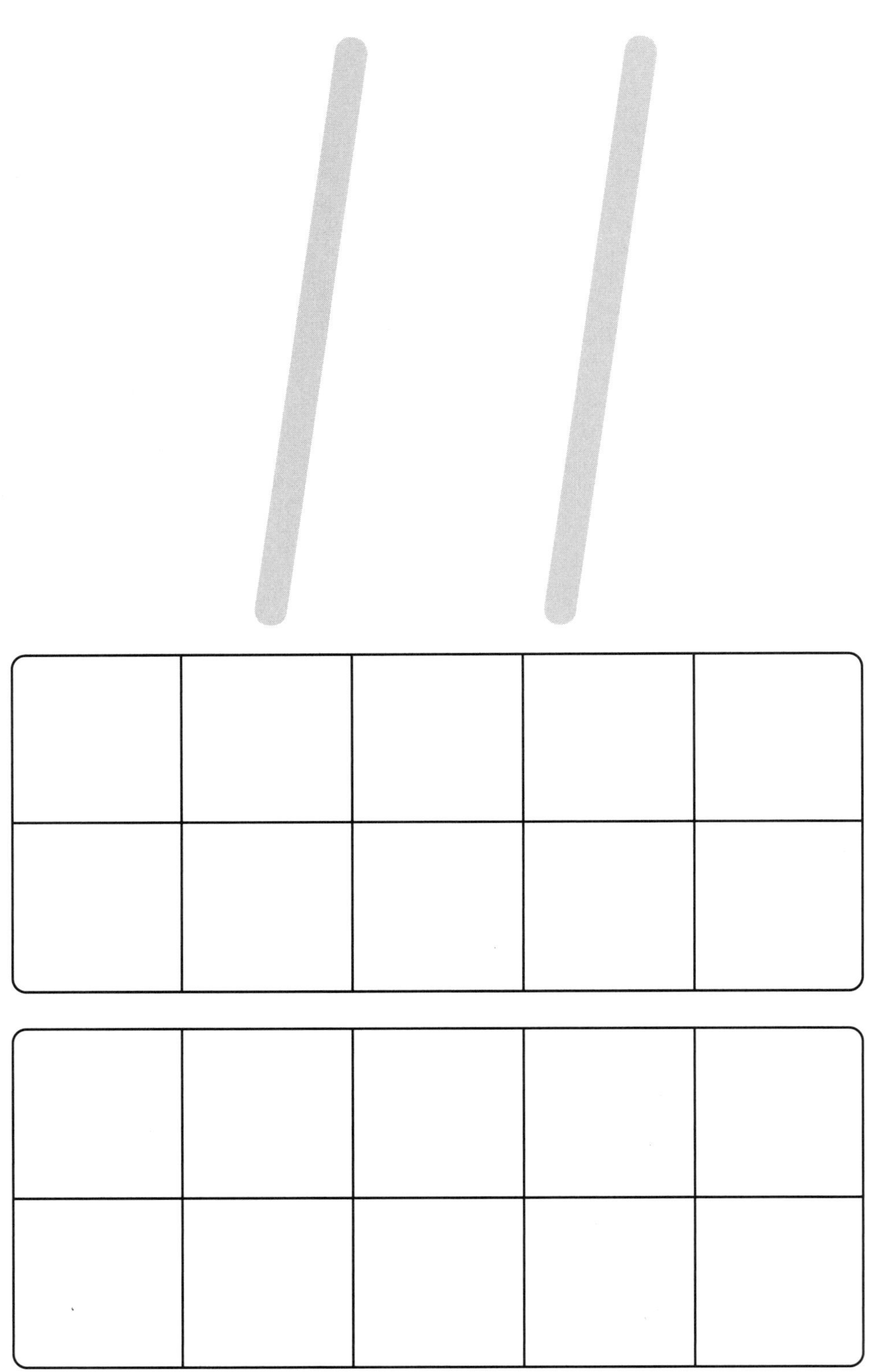

Channel.

Trace over.

Trace over.

Colour 11 cricket caps.

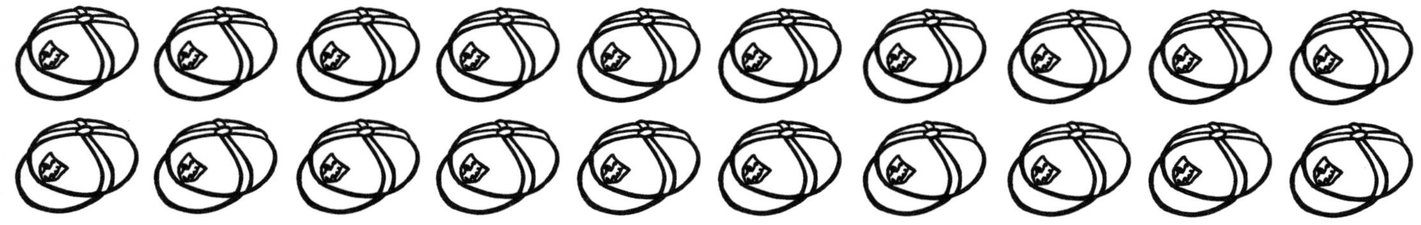

Colour the 11th bat orange.

Channel.

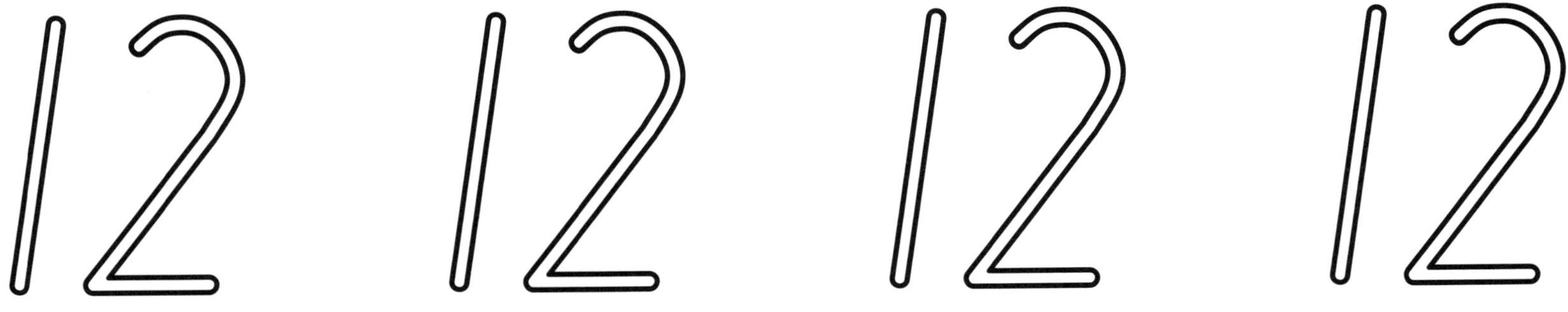

Trace over.

12 12 12 12

Trace over.

twelve twelve

Colour 12 eggs.

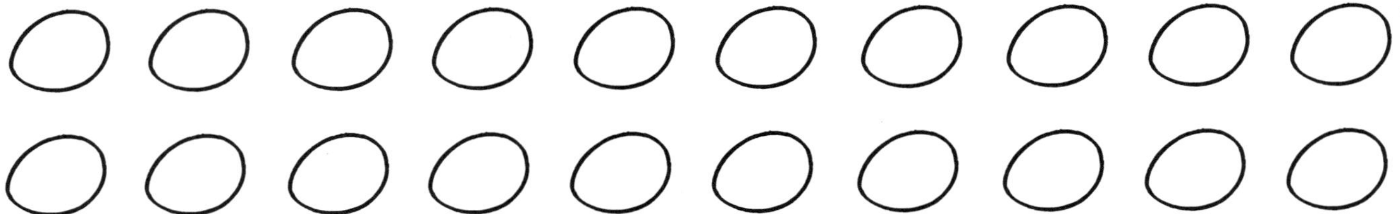

Colour the 12th chick yellow.

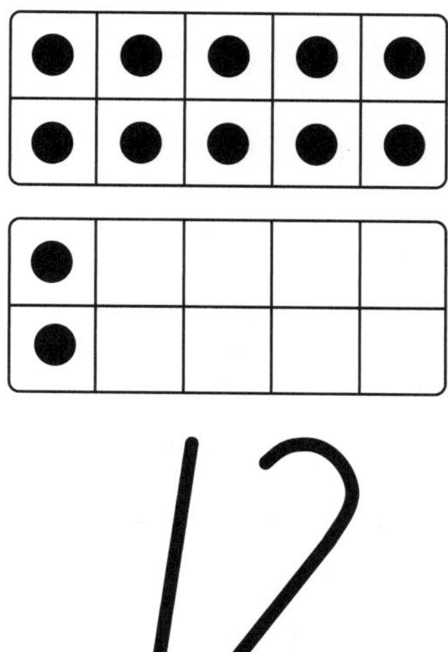
12

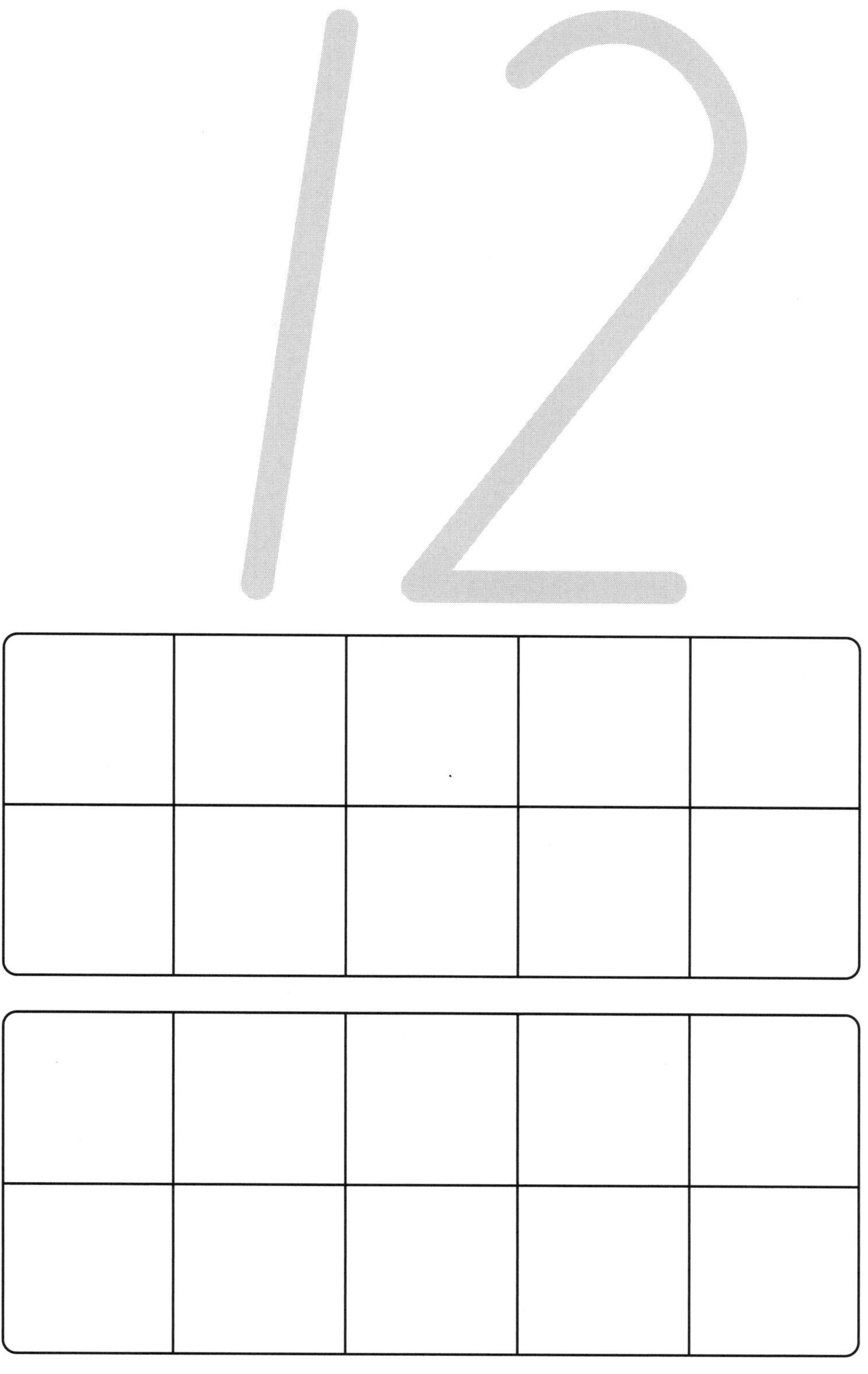
12

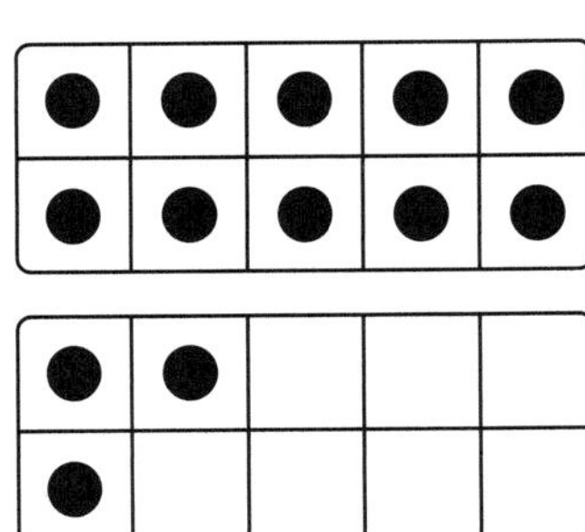

13

Channel.

13 13 13 13

Trace over.

13 13 13 13

Trace over.

thirteen thirteen

Colour 13 apples.

Colour the 13th pear green.

Channel.

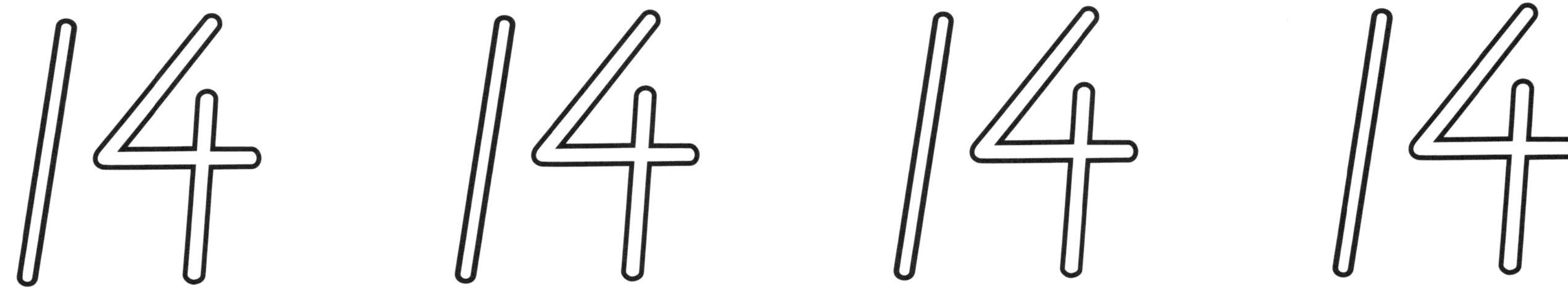

Trace over.

14 14 14 14

Trace over.

fourteen fourteen

Colour 14 bikes.

Colour the 14th scooter blue.

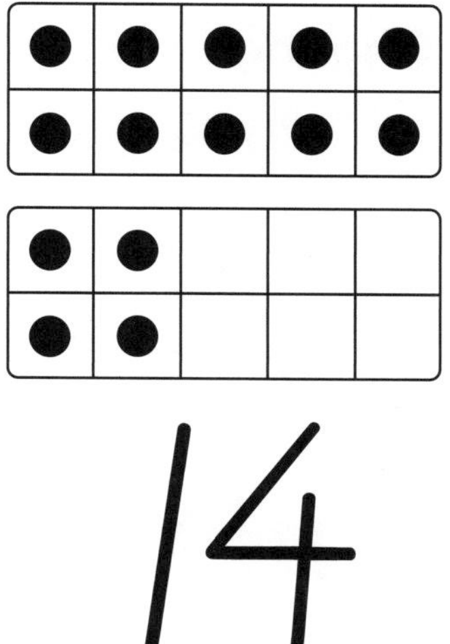
14

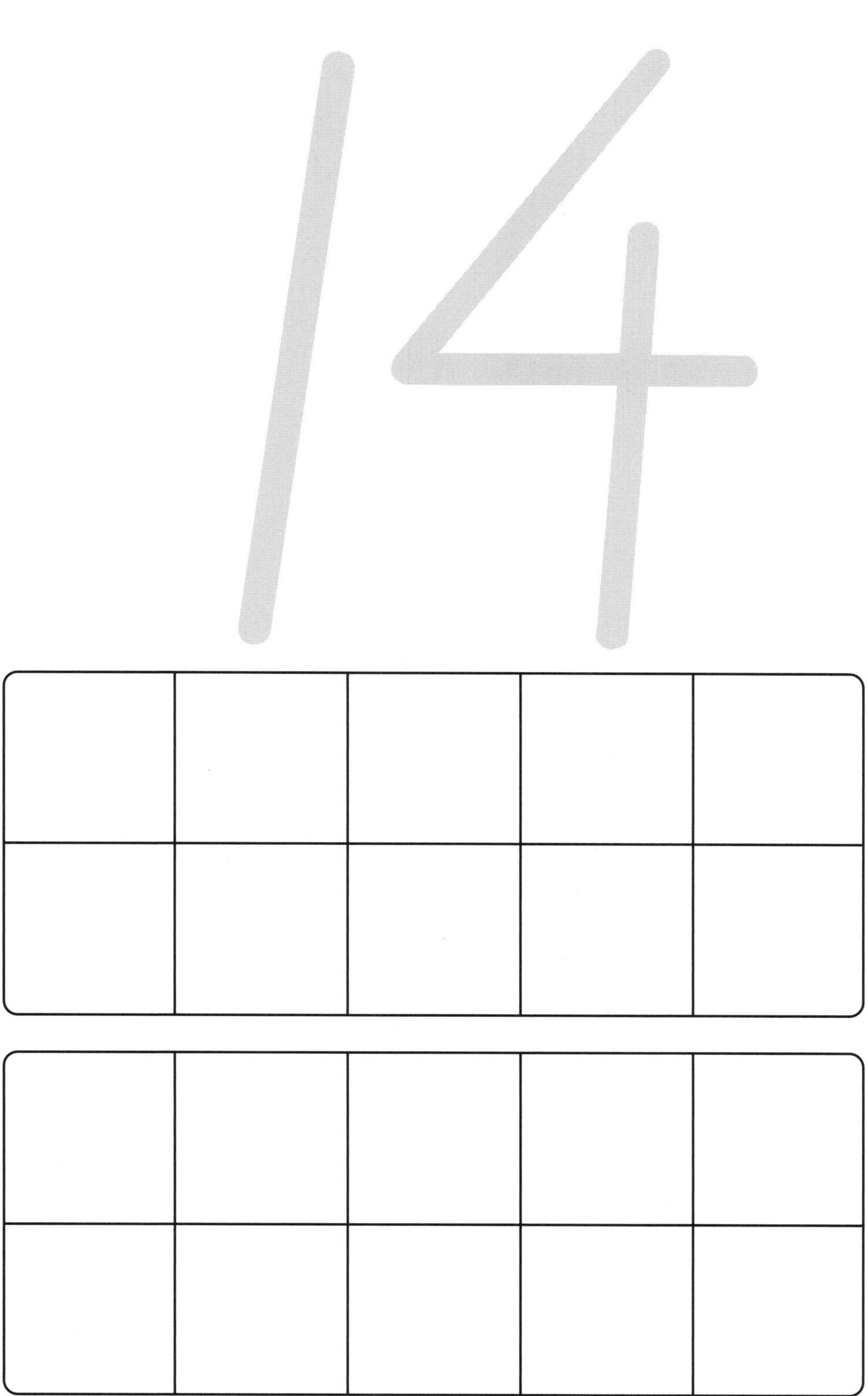
14

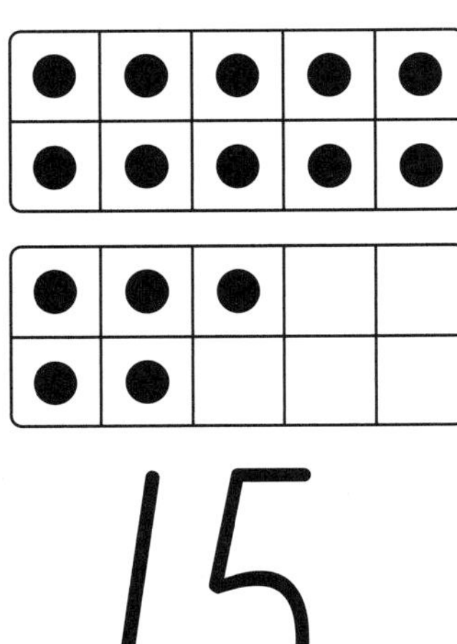

15

Channel.

15 15 15 15

Trace over.

15 15 15 15

Trace over.

fifteen fifteen

Colour 15 hands.

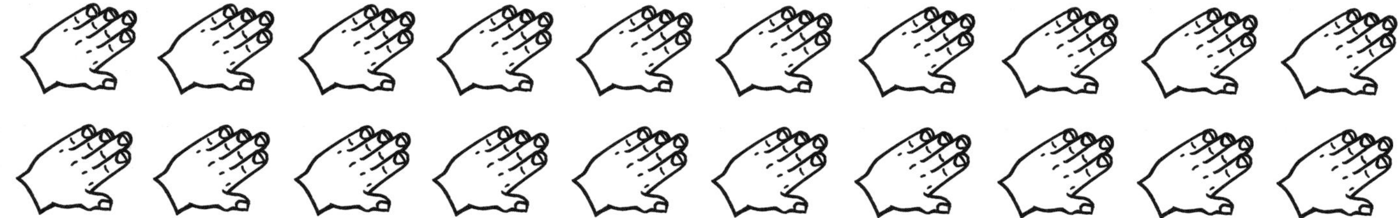

Colour the 15th starfish red.

Channel.

16 16 16 16

Trace over.

16 16 16 16

Trace over.

sixteen sixteen

Colour 16 cats.

Colour the 16th dog black.

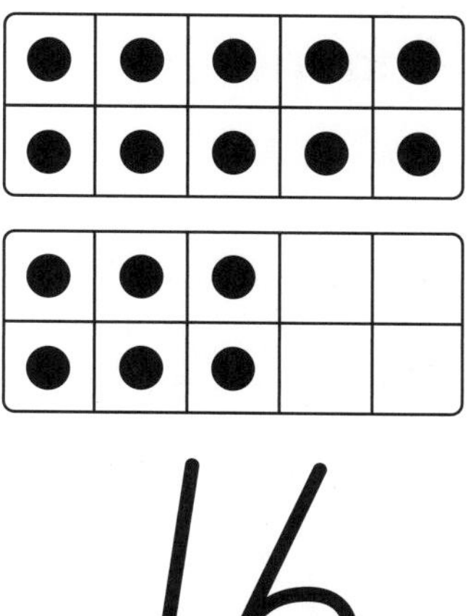
16

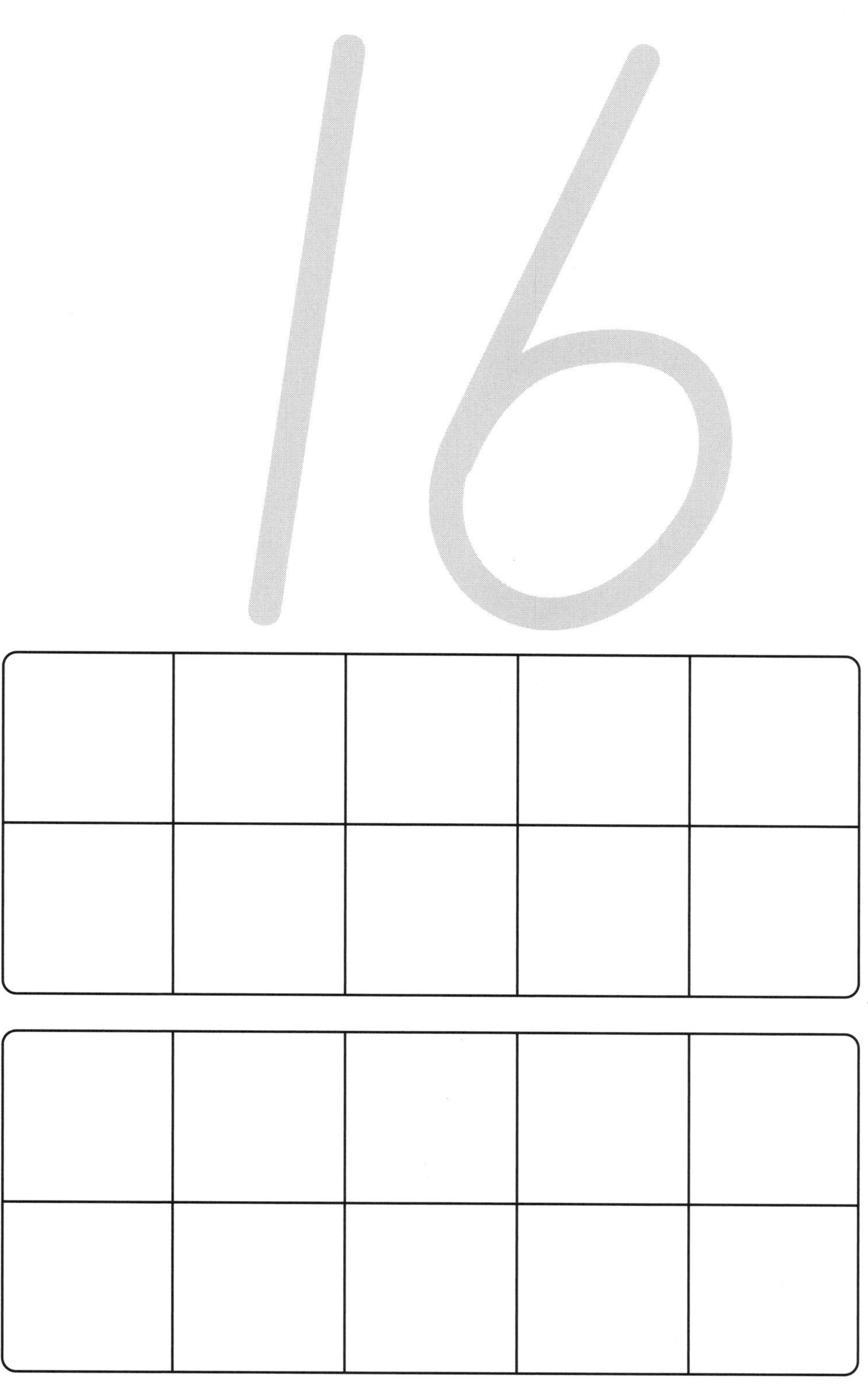
16

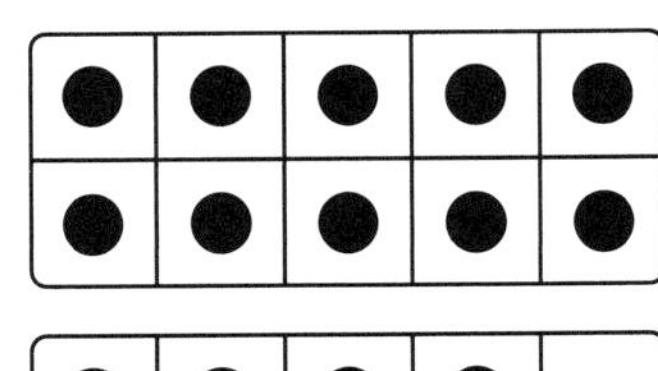
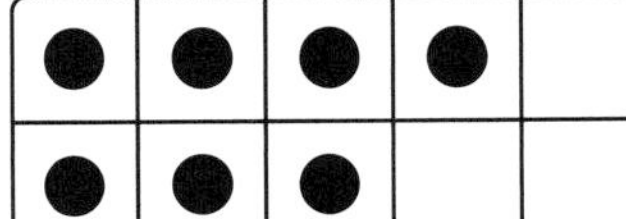

17

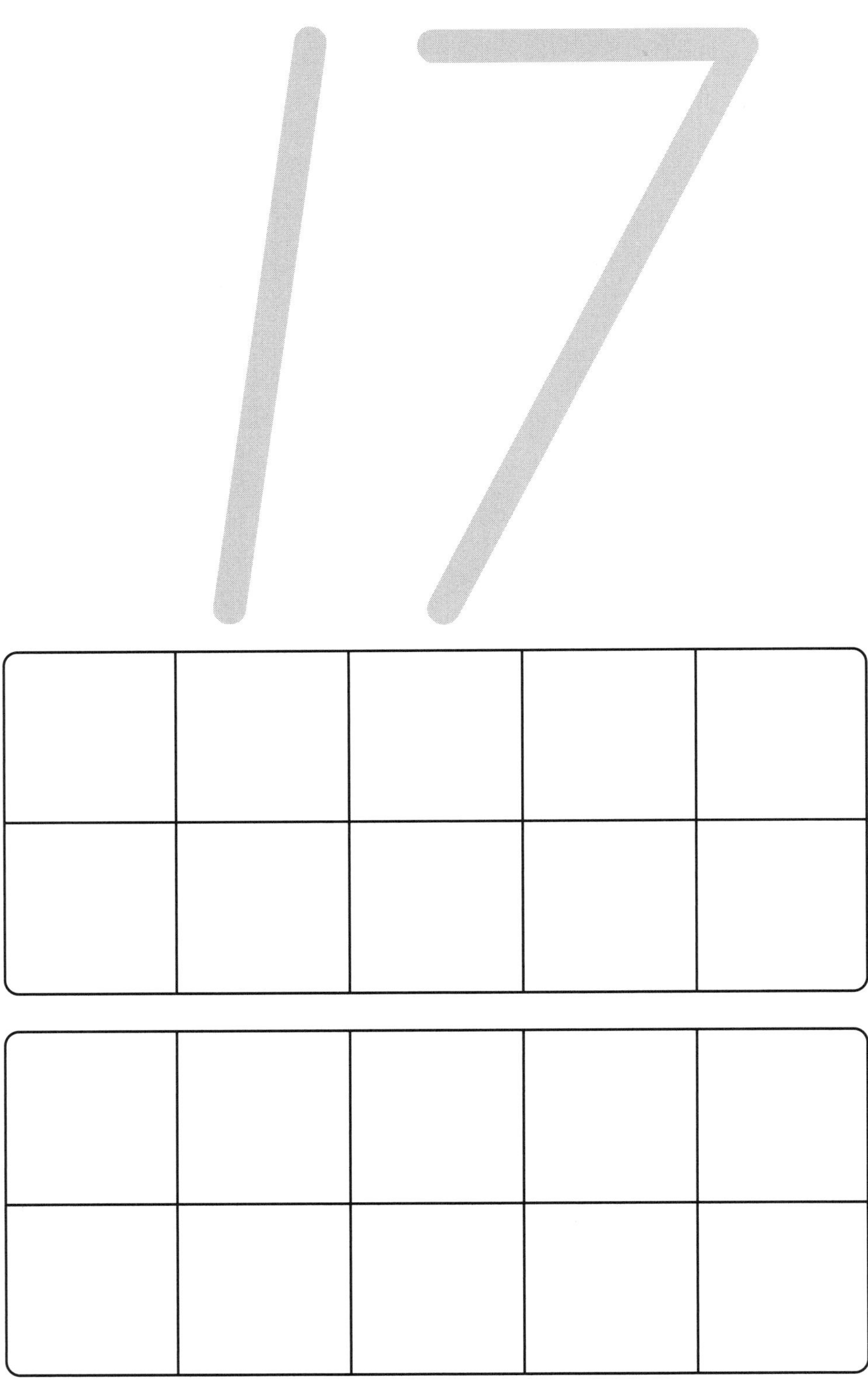

Channel.

Trace over.

17 17 17 17

Trace over.

seventeen seventeen

Colour 17 clovers.

Colour the 17th leaf green.

Channel.

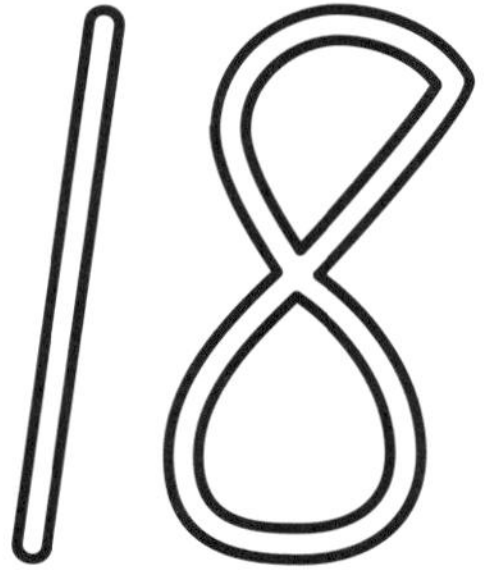
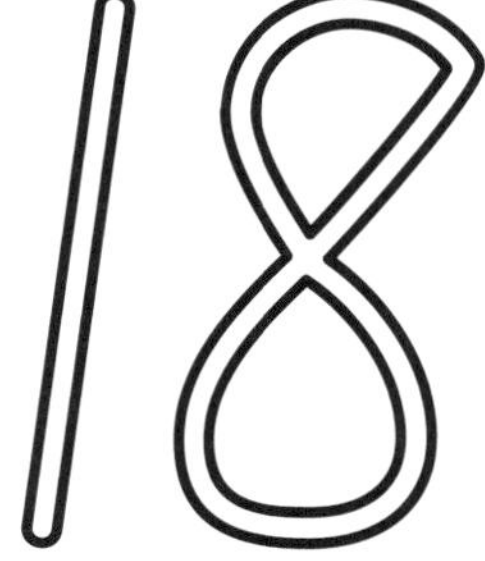
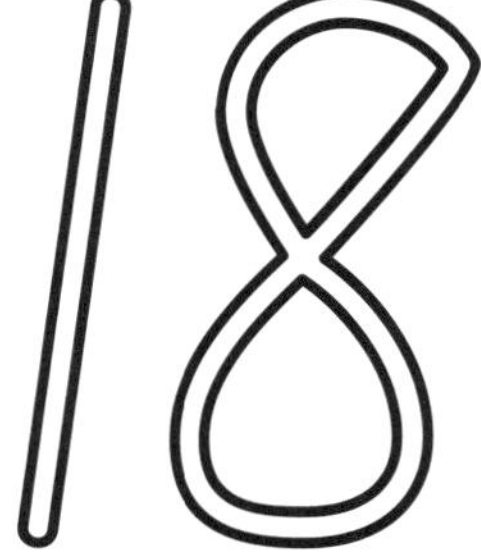
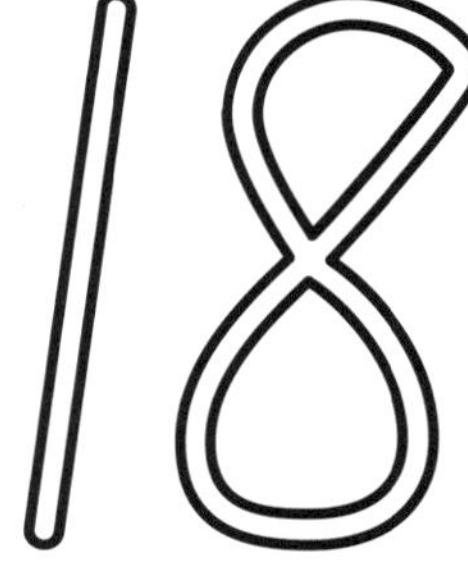

Trace over.

18 18 18 18

Trace over.

eighteen eighteen

Colour 18 ants.

Colour the 18th bee yellow.

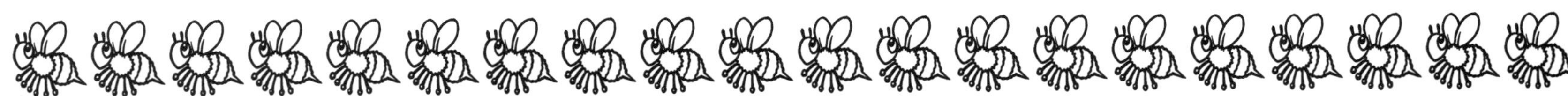

18

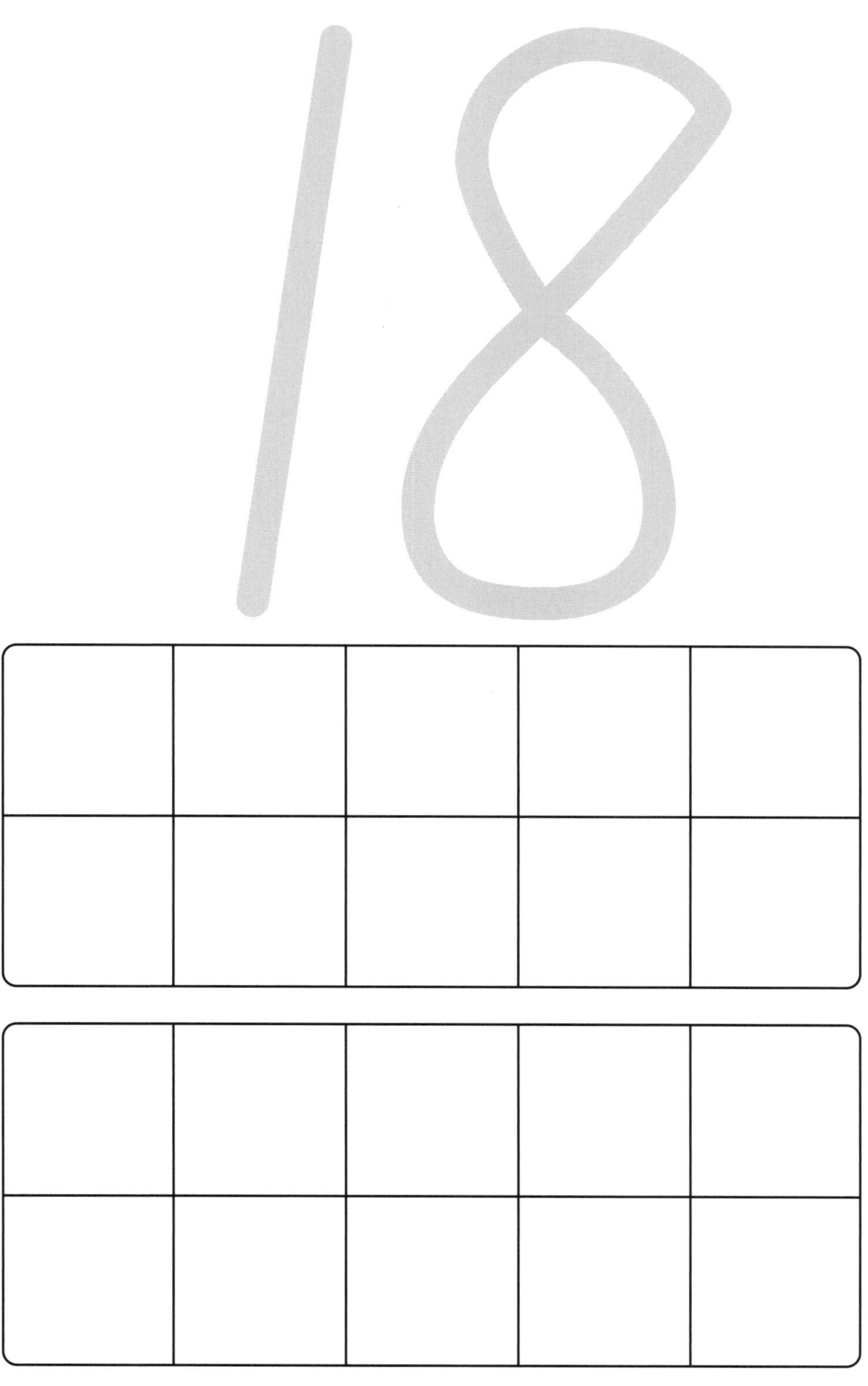
18

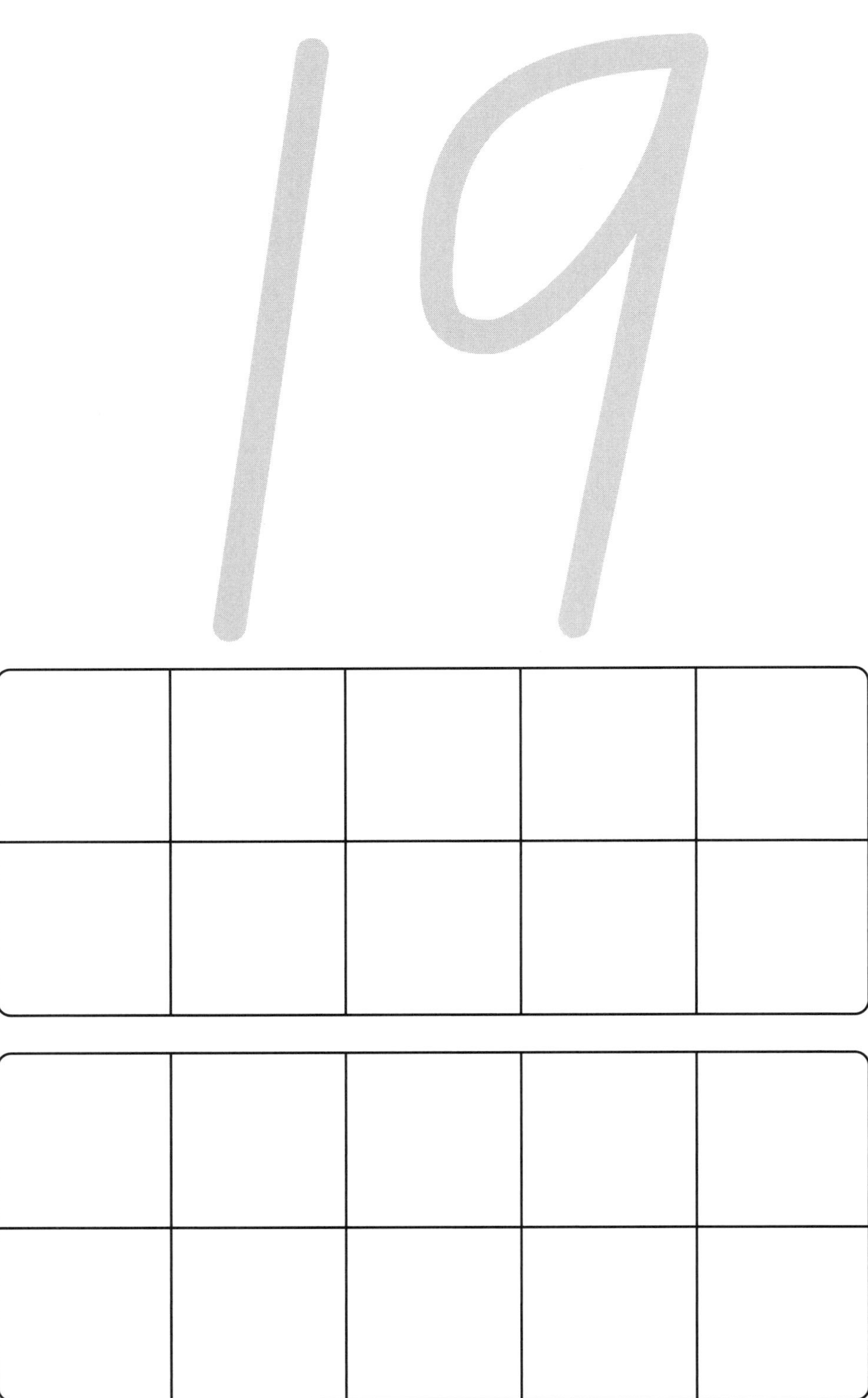

Channel.

19 19 19 19

Trace over.

19 19 19 19

Trace over.

nineteen nineteen

Colour 19 jellyfish.

Colour the 19th seahorse orange.

Channel.

Trace over.

20 20 20

Trace over.

twenty twenty

Colour 20 ice-creams.

Colour the 20th cup cake pink.

20

20

Colour:

- 2 children
- 6 spiders black
- 5 ants green
- 9 flowers red
- 4 cats brown
- 14 apples red
- 16 bees yellow